STAND UP & FLIP OVER · COOKBOOKS ·

sufo

RECIPES FROM

Northern
ITALY

NORTHERN ITALY – INDEX

CONTENTS

MASCARPONE AND COFFEE PUDDING
Tiramisu

Preparation
20 minutes

Refrigerate
4 hours

Serves 6

We recommend you use a transparent dish (glass or otherwise) as the dessert is served in the dish it is prepared in, and it is nice to see the various layers. Instant coffee can be used, but the taste of real coffee is unbeatable.

5 fl oz (150 ml) strong black coffee

3 eggs (size 3), separated

3 tablespoons caster sugar

9 oz (250 g) mascarpone cheese

4 tablespoons of any liqueur of your choice (such as brandy or dark rum)

26-32 sponge fingers

Cocoa powder

Make the strong black coffee and leave it to cool.

In a bowl, beat the egg yolks and the sugar until pale, light and creamy.

Soften the mascarpone cheese in a bowl and gradually stir in the egg yolk mixture.

Whisk the egg whites with a pinch of salt until stiff, then gently fold into the mascarpone mixture with a metal spoon.

Mix the cooled coffee with the liqueur and quickly dip both sides of each sponge finger into the liquid. Arrange them in a layer in the bottom of a 2 pint (1.15 litre) dish, and spoon some of the mascarpone mixture over the biscuits. Sprinkle a fine layer of cocoa powder over the top.

Continue with layers of dipped sponge fingers, mascarpone mixture and a fine layer of cocoa powder, until all the ingredients are used up.

Finish with a layer of mascarpone and sprinkle the top with a fine layer of cocoa powder. Refrigerate for at least 3 to 4 hours before serving.

NORTHERN ITALY

Northern Italy is a vast and varied land, the top of the boot that incorporates landlocked regions, mountains and soft rolling hills, lakes and rivers and seaside towns. Until the unification in 1861, Italy was made up of independent states, each divided culturally and gastronomically, which is perhaps why these regions are still today quite distinctly different from one another, each boasting its own specialities, delicacies, ingredients, cooking methods and culinary influences.

The North of Italy is home to the world famous white truffle, Parmesan cheese, Parma ham, balsamic vinegar, Barolo and Chianti wines and of course, it produces some of the finest olive oils in the world.

The recipes for this book have been chosen to demonstrate the versatility of Italian food and the diversity of regional cooking. These recipes have been thoroughly researched, sometimes simplified or adapted to today's taste and way of life and then carefully tested and "tasted". The ingredients have also been carefully researched for availability and alternatives suggested where appropriate, while still retaining authenticity and the true essence of the dish.

The culinary journey starts in the north west region of Piedmont, which stretches from the Italian Alps to the Po Valley. It is where elegant and sophisticated food, influenced by the French, shares the table with more humble peasant food. But overall the food is rich, with butter, cream and cheese playing a major role. Trout from the Alpine streams is cooked with red wine, veal and a lot of offal is widely eaten, but perhaps its greatest claim to fame is that it is home to the city of Alba where the great white truffle is hunted. The pungent scent of the truffle pervades most of the dishes, along with garlic and cream and wine. For it is here too that most of the DOC wines are produced, Barbera, Barolo and Asti Spumante.

The neighbouring region of Lombardy, is where salami come into their own, it has some of the finest meats in the country and polenta takes the place of pasta. From the region's capital city Milan comes ossobucco - the shin of veal and marrow bone, cooked in white wine, and served with gremolada, a mixture of lemon rind, garlic and parsley, for authenticity. Risotto alla Milanese is another typical dish from this region; after all this is where half the country's rice is grown.

Below Piedmont, Liguria hugs the coast and relies more heavily on the sea for its food – fish, such as sardines, mackerel and anchovies play a prominent part of the cooking.

But its perfect climate of cool summer and mild winters means that vegetables and herbs grow in profusion here and it is hardly surprising to find that it is from here that the ubiquitous basil pesto originated.

Travelling further east and onto the Adriatic coast to Veneto, the cooking takes another turn. Here the food reflects the elegance of the town of Venice. Fish come into their own, squid is a speciality and fresh herbs and spices are more widely used. Risi e Bisi is a classic dish from this region that dates back to the days of the Doges of Venice. Polenta is also a very important element of the cooking of Veneto as corn was imported by the Venetians and later cultivated in the Po delta.

Renowned as the richest gastronomic region in Italy, Emilia Romagna lies between the Ligurian sea and the Adriatic. The town of Parma is birthplace to the celebrated cheese Parmesan and the specially dried and cured Parma ham. Bologna, capital of Emilia Romagna, lays claim to yet another of Italy's famous exports – Bolognese sauce for pasta. From the rich town of Modena comes the delicious dark-coloured balsamic vinegar made from Trebbiano grapes.

Tuscany, which is just below Emilia Romagna, is perhaps best described as the land of olive groves and vineyards, where the cooking is more rustic, with the accent on fresh vegetables and beans used in hearty soups and stews and often combined with tomatoes and garlic.

Although a landlocked region, neighbouring Umbria is rich in rivers and lakes and fish are commonly found on the menus here. But perhaps it is better known as home of the black truffle and pork, two ingredients found most commonly in the region's kitchens.

The region of Le Marche, neatly hems Umbria in, and follows the Adriatic coast. It is green and lush, made up of mountains and valleys, where vines and some of the finest olives grow. And because of its proximity to the sea, fish and shellfish dominate the cooking, often served in delicious soups and stews. The region's wine Verdicchio has also, justly won, world-wide acclaim.

With dishes such as these and ingredients so fine, is it any wonder that food plays such a large part of Italian life, from the ritual of preparation to the huge occasion of sitting down with the family at the table? The cooking is so varied, influenced by the Romans to Byzantines, Arabs, French and Spanish, that to pass Italy off as the land of pizza and pasta is a great crime - it has so much more to offer.

CHILLED CHOCOLATE CAKE
Dolce Torinese

Preparation
30 minutes

Refrigerate
overnight

Serves 6 to 8

8 oz (225 g) plain chocolate, cut into small cubes

4 fl oz (120 ml) rum

8 oz (225 g) butter, softened

2 oz (50 g) caster sugar

2 eggs (size 3), separated

5 oz (150 g) blanched almonds, finely chopped

Pinch of salt

10-12 butter biscuits (such as French Petit Beurre or tea biscuits), broken into small pieces

Icing sugar for sprinkling

Double cream, whipped (optional)

Grease a 2 to 2½ pint (1 to 1.4 l) loaf tin with vegetable oil and turn it upside down on kitchen paper to drain the excess oil.

In a heavy saucepan, let the chocolate melt on very low heat. When it has melted, slowly add the rum, stirring all the time.

Remove from the heat and allow to cool to room temperature.

In a large mixing bowl, beat the softened butter until pale and creamy. Beat in the sugar and the egg yolks, one by one. Add the chopped almonds and cooled chocolate mixture.

In another bowl, beat the egg whites with a pinch of salt until stiff. Fold them carefully into the chocolate mixture, then very gently fold in the broken biscuits, discarding the crumbs. Fill the greased loaf tin with the mixture and smooth the top with a rubber spatula.

Cover with plastic film and keep in the refrigerator, preferably overnight.

When serving, run the blade of a knife around the sides and plunge the bottom of the loaf tin into hot water for a few seconds. Then quickly turn the tin onto a chilled dish and tap lightly. If necessary, repeat the procedure until the cake slides out easily. Return to the refrigerator until ready to serve.

Sieve icing sugar on top and serve, with whipped cream if desired.

SELECTION OF COLD MEATS WITH ROASTED GARLIC

Antipasto misto con aglio arrosto

⏱ Preparation
15 minutes

🕐 Cooking
1 hour

Serves 6

The term antipasto literally means "before the pasta" and refers to a selection of sliced meats and salami, fish, olives, raw and marinated vegetables, and salads – in fact an Italian Hors-d'oeuvres.

6 slices of mortadella

12 slices of Parma ham

6 slices of 3 different salami (making 18 in all)

6 slices of Coppa ham

6 whole artichoke hearts in oil

Green and black olives

For the roasted garlic:

6 whole bulbs of garlic

2 tablespoons olive oil

1 teaspoon tomato purée

4 fl oz (120 ml) water

Salt and freshly ground black pepper

Arrange the meats on a large oval platter and garnish with the artichoke hearts, olives and roasted garlic.

To roast the garlic, pull any untidy or loose pieces of the outer skin off the garlic, leaving the bulbs intact. Cut the tops off about ½ inch (1 cm) down to expose the garlic flesh.

Drop the bulbs into salted boiling water and cook for 5 minutes. Drain and place them in a small baking dish. Pour over the oil and the tomato purée diluted with the 4 fl oz (120 ml) of water. Season with salt and pepper to taste.

Preheat the oven to 375°F/190°C/Gas 5.

Cover the baking dish with foil and bake in the oven for 1 hour. From time to time, remove the dish from the oven, take off the foil, baste the garlic with the juices, cover again and put back in the oven. If the liquid in the baking dish starts to dry up, add a little more water.

Allow to cool and use the whole garlic bulbs to garnish the Antipasto misto.

Serve with fresh crusty bread or ciabatta.

MARINATED SARDINES
Sardine marinate

	Preparation 30 minutes	Marinate 12 hours
	Cooking 20 minutes	Serves 4 to 6

1-1½ lb (450-650 g) fresh sardines

Plain flour

Vegetable oil for frying

Salt and freshly ground black pepper

1 medium-sized sweet red onion, thinly sliced

1 medium-sized spanish onion, thinly sliced

4 fl oz (120 ml) white wine vinegar

4-6 bay leaves

Gut and scale the sardines and remove the bone. Wash them in cold water and pat dry with kitchen paper.

Dip each sardine in flour and shake off the excess flour.

Pour the oil into a large frying pan, to about ½inch (1 cm) depth. When the oil is hot, place the sardines in the pan, without crowding them. Fry for about 2 to 4 minutes on each side (depending on their size), or until they are brown and crisp.

With a slotted spoon, remove the fish from the pan and place in a shallow serving dish, big enough to take all the sardines in a single layer without overlapping them. Sprinkle with salt and pepper to taste.

Discard half the oil in the pan. Reheat the remaining oil, put in the slices of onion and cook on a medium to low heat, stirring occasionally, until they are soft but not coloured.

Add the vinegar, turn up the heat and boil for 1 minute, stirring all the time. Then pour the contents of the pan over the sardines, spreading the onions evenly over the fish. Place the bay leaves on top and cover with foil.

Leave the sardines in the marinade for at least 12 hours. They will keep in the refrigerator for several days. Remove them from the refrigerator 1 hour before serving.

ASPARAGUS WITH PARMESAN CHEESE
Asparagi alla Parmigiana

 Preparation
5 minutes

 Cooking
20 minutes **Serves 4**

Asparagus are plentiful and highly regarded in Italy. They can be served hot, as in this recipe, placed alongside a fried egg to dip into the yolk, or cooked and served cold with mayonnaise or simply dressed with oil and lemon.

2 lb (900 g) asparagus

4 tablespoons freshly grated Parmesan

6 oz (175 g) unsalted butter

Cut the woody ends off the asparagus and trim to an even length.

Put the asparagus into boiling salted water and cook them for 10 to 15 minutes, until just tender. Drain and divide them between 4 plates. Sprinkle the Parmesan over the tips and half way up the stalks.

Have the butter ready in a little pan and heat it until it turns brown.

Pour the butter, sizzling and foaming, over the asparagus and serve immediately.

AUBERGINE PARMA-STYLE
Parmigiana di melanzane

 Preparation
1 hour

 Cooking
1 hour 15 mins **Serves 4**

Aubergines soak up a lot of oil, therefore you may need to replenish the oil in the pan while frying the aubergine slices.

6 medium-sized aubergines

Salt

Olive oil for frying

4-6 oz (100-175 g) Parma ham, thinly sliced

½ pint (300 ml) rich tomato sauce (see page 26)

Freshly ground black pepper to taste

4 oz (100 g) grated Parmesan

2 oz (50 g) butter

Wash and trim the aubergines, cut them into ½ inch (1 cm) thick slices. Sprinkle them with salt and leave in a colander for about 1 hour to allow the bitter juices to drain off. Then rinse the slices thoroughly and pat them dry with kitchen paper.

Heat the olive oil in a large frying pan and fry the aubergine slices, in several batches if necessary, on both sides, until golden brown. Drain them on kitchen paper.

Preheat the oven to 325°F/160°C/Gas 3. Butter an ovenproof dish and place a layer of aubergine slices. Cover with slices of Parma ham and spoon over some of the tomato sauce. Sprinkle with pepper to taste and Parmesan. Repeat the layers until all the ingredients are used up, finishing with a layer of Parmesan. Dot the top with pieces of butter and cook in a moderate oven for about 45 minutes to 1 hour. Serve hot.

TUNA AND BEAN SALAD
Insalata di tonno e fagioli

Preparation
30 minutes

Serves 4 to 6

4 oz (100 g) tomatoes, diced very small

4 oz (100 g) cucumber, finely diced

6-8 spring onions or 1 small onion, finely diced

1 green pepper, seeded and finely diced

1 garlic clove, peeled and crushed

1 lb (450 g) cooked or tinned berlotti beans

1 x 7 oz (200 g) can tuna

4-6 tablespoons mayonnaise (see page 25)

Salt and freshly ground black pepper

Put the tomatoes, cucumber, onions, green pepper and garlic into a bowl.

Mash ¾ of the beans with a fork and add to the bowl, with the remaining whole beans.

Add the drained tuna, flaking it into small pieces.

Mix all the ingredients together with 4 tablespoons of the mayonnaise, adding more, if necessary, until a creamy consistency is achieved.

Serve on a bed of lettuce leaves. Do not season with salt and pepper until you are ready to serve and do not make the salad too far in advance.

SPINACH RISSOLES
Polpettine al spinaci

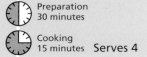
Preparation
30 minutes

Cooking
15 minutes   Serves 4

1 lb (450 g) cooked spinach

1 lb (450 g) spicy Italian sausage

2 eggs (size 3), lightly beaten

Salt and freshly ground black pepper

4 tablespoons oil for frying

6 oz (175 g) butter

1 clove garlic, peeled and crushed

½ tablespoon finely chopped fresh parsley

Squeeze all the moisture out of the spinach, chop finely and place in a bowl.

Remove the sausage meat from its skin and add to the spinach with the 2 eggs. Season to taste and mix well.

Divide the mixture into 8 portions, forming each one into a ball. Roll each ball in the flour, then flatten to make the rissoles. Shake off the excess flour.

Heat the oil in a pan and gently fry the rissoles for about 3 to 4

minutes each side, or until they are brown and cooked through. Remove them from the pan, drain on kitchen paper and keep them warm in a low oven, covered with foil.

Heat the butter in a small pan, add the garlic and parsley and cook for 1 minute.

To serve, put 2 rissoles on each plate and pour over the hot butter sauce.

SPICY BROCCOLI AND CAULIFLOWER
Broccoli e cavolfiore piccante

Preparation 10 minutes

Cooking 15 minutes Serves 4

Chillies come in various shapes and sizes. Usually, the smaller they are the hotter they taste. The dried red ones available in most shops or supermarkets are quite powerful, so experiment with a small chilli, or even half a chilli, until you get to know their strength.

½ lb (225 g) cauliflower florets, trimmed

½ lb (225 g) broccoli florets, trimmed

3 tablespoons olive oil

1 oz (25 g) butter

½ dried red chilli,crumbled
or
½ teaspoon crushed chillies

2 garlic cloves , peeled and cut into thin slivers

Salt and freshly ground black pepper

Drop the cauliflower florets into boiling salted water, bring back to the boil and cook for 3 minutes. Then add the broccoli florets, and cook for a further 3 minutes, or until just tender, but still crisp. Rinse them under cold running water to stop them cooking, then drain.

Heat the oil and butter in a large frying pan, add the crumbled chilli or crushed chillies and the garlic slivers, and cook on a low heat until the garlic starts to colour.

Add the drained cauliflower and broccoli florets and cook for about 5 minutes, turning them gently every now and again. Season to taste and serve.

POTATOES WITH CREAM AND HERBS
Patate alla crema

Preparation 15 minutes

Cooking 25 minutes Serves 4 to 6

8-10 medium-sized potatoes, washed

4 oz (100 g) butter or a mixture of butter and oil

1 medium-sized onion, peeled and chopped

3 tablespoons chopped fresh parsley

3 tablespoons chopped fresh mint

Salt and freshly ground black pepper

10 fl oz (300 ml) single cream

2 tablespoons chopped fresh parsley to garnish

Boil the potatoes in their skin for 15 to 20 minutes. Do not overcook them. Drain the potatoes and leave them to cool, then peel and chop them into small cubes.

In a deep frying pan, melt the butter, (or butter and oil), add the onion, parsley, mint, salt and pepper to taste. Mix well, cover and cook on a low heat for a few minutes, until the onion is cooked but not coloured.

Remove the lid, add the potatoes, mix well to coat them with the butter mixture. Then add the cream and shake the pan until the cream bubbles. Sprinkle with chopped parsley and serve immediately.

GRILLED VEGETABLES
Verdure alla griglia

 Preparation
30 minutes

 Cooking
20 minutes   Serves 4 to 6

1 large or 2 small aubergines

2 courgettes

1 head of radicchio

4 red peppers,(or 2 red and 2 yellow),
peeled (see page 24), cored and seeded

4-8 spring onions

Olive oil for basting

4 garlic cloves, peeled and finely chopped

Salt and freshly ground black pepper

2 tablespoons finely chopped fresh parsley

6 tablespoons of virgin olive oil

Heat a cast iron grill until very hot.

While the grill is heating, cut the aubergines into ½inch (1cm) thick slices.

Cut the courgettes into thin slices, lengthwise, on a mandolin or with a very sharp knife.

Cut the radicchio head into 4 equal portions, cut the peppers in half, and trim the spring onions.

Put some olive oil in a small bowl and, when the grill is hot, brush the aubergine slices on both sides with a pastry brush dipped into the oil. Place them on the hot grill. After 3 minutes, turn them over with a fish slice, brush with oil again and grill for a further 3 minutes. When the slices are cooked, remove from the grill and set aside.

Brush the courgette slices with oil and grill in the same way for about 2 minutes on each side.

Brush the radicchio quarters with oil, put them on the grill, fanning and flattening them out with a fish slice or a metal spatula. Grill them for 2 minutes on each side.

Brush the peppers with oil and grill for 2 minutes either side.

Lastly, oil and grill the spring onions for 3 minutes either side.

Arrange the grilled vegetables on a large platter. Season with salt and pepper. Scatter the garlic and the parsley over the vegetables. Spoon over the virgin olive oil and serve with fresh crusty white bread.

SPINACH SOUFFLE
Sformato di spinaci

 Preparation
20 minutes

Cooking
30 minutes   Serves 4

2 lb (900 g) fresh spinach leaves, stems removed

2 oz (50 g) butter

2 oz (50 g) plain flour

¼ pint (150 ml) single cream

Salt and freshly ground black pepper

1 teaspoon freshly grated nutmeg

2 egg yolks (size 3)

3 egg whites (size 3)

Freshly grated Parmesan

Wash the spinach leaves in cold water and cook them for 6 to 8 minutes, in a large covered pan, with 1 teaspoon of salt and only the water clinging to the leaves. Drain and chop coarsely.

In a heavy saucepan, gently melt the butter, then add the flour. Mix well and cook, on a low heat, for 2 minutes.

Add the cream and bring to the boil. Season with salt, pepper and nutmeg, then take off the heat.

In a bowl beat the egg yolks with a fork and gradually stir them into the cream mixture. Add the coarsely chopped spinach, mix well and leave aside to cool.

Whisk the egg whites with a pinch of salt until stiff and gently fold them into the cooled spinach mixture.

Preheat the oven to 375°F/190°C/Gas 5

Half fill a 2 pint (1 litre) buttered soufflé dish (or individual ramekins) with the spinach mixture. Sprinkle with freshly grated Parmesan, and bake in the oven for 15 to 20 minutes, until the soufflé has risen and browned on top. Serve immediately. It is also very nice cold.

(If you are using individual ramekins, reduce the cooking time by about 5 minutes.)

TUSCAN BEAN SOUP
La Ribollita

Preparation 30 minutes	Soak overnight
Cooking 2 hours	Serves 4

Ribollita means "boiled again", and this soup is improved by being made in advance and gently reheated. In this recipe, we suggest a dark green cabbage to replace the cavolo nero, seldom found outside Tuscany. This is a thick peasant soup – a meal in itself.

12 oz (350 g) dried cannellini or white haricot beans, soaked overnight

8 tablespoons olive oil

2 celery stalks, finely chopped

2 large carrots, peeled and finely chopped

2 leeks, finely chopped

4 large ripe tomatoes, peeled (see page 24), seeded and chopped

3 sprigs thyme

3 garlic cloves, peeled

8 oz (225 g) dark green cabbage, finely sliced

Salt and freshly ground black pepper

1 red onion, finely sliced
or
6 spring onions, finely chopped

Virgin olive oil

Drain the beans and place in a large pan in plenty of water and cook, covered, until almost tender. Remove from the heat and set aside for 1 hour, then drain the beans, reserving the liquid.

Purée ¾ of the beans with an equal amount of fresh water. Set aside the remainder of the beans.

Heat the oil in a large pan and fry the celery, carrots and leeks for about 5 minutes, or until tender. Add the tomatoes, thyme, garlic and stir well. Then add the cabbage and season to taste.

Cover and cook slowly for about 10 minutes. Then add the bean purée, adding some of the bean water if the soup is too thick.

Cover and cook slowly for about 1 hour, thinning with more bean water or hot water if the soup is still too thick.

About 10 minutes before the end of cooking time, add the whole beans previously set aside and adjust the seasoning.

Serve with a bowl of chopped red onions or spring onions, and sprinkle some virgin olive oil over the top of the soup.

MEAT LOAF
Polpettone

2 lb (900 g) mixed minced meat, (veal, pork and beef)

4 oz (100 g) freshly grated Parmesan

4 oz (100 g) fresh breadcrumbs (see page 24)

1 large onion, peeled and finely chopped

1 tablespoon finely chopped fresh parsley

2 garlic cloves, peeled and crushed

1 sprig rosemary, finely chopped

1 pinch of grated nutmeg

4 eggs (size 3)

Salt and freshly ground black pepper

Put the minced meats, Parmesan, breadcrumbs, onion, parsley, garlic, rosemary and nutmeg in a large bowl, and season to taste. Break in the eggs and mix thoroughly with your hands.

Preheat the oven to 350°F/180°C/Gas 4

Put the mixture in a 2 lb (900 g) buttered loaf tin and bake in the oven for 45 minutes.

Take the loaf tin out of the oven and invert the meat loaf and all its juices on to a baking tray and return to the oven for a further 30 to 40 minutes, so it can brown on the top.

You can add a few spoonfuls of water to the juices in the baking tray to prevent them burning or drying.

Serve with a rich tomato sauce (see page 26).

CHICKEN SOUP
zuppa di pollo

 Preparation
10 minutes

Cooking
5 minutes Serves 4

8 oz (225 g) boneless chicken breast, cooked and skinned

3 egg yolks (size 3)

Salt and freshly ground black pepper

Freshly grated nutmeg to taste

4 tablespoons of freshly grated Parmesan

1½ pints (850 ml) home-made chicken stock

Chop the cooked chicken finely.

Put the egg yolks in a bowl and whisk. Add the chopped chicken, salt and pepper, nutmeg, and mix well, mashing the chicken slightly with a fork. Then add the Parmesan.

Bring the chicken stock to the boil and pour onto the chicken and Parmesan mixture, stirring quickly for 2 to 3 minutes.

Serve immediately with crisp slices of toast or a loaf of fresh crusty bread.

BREAD AND TOMATO SOUP
Pappa al pomodoro

 Preparation
20 minutes

Cooking
1 hour 15 mins Serves 6

This is a really satisfying soup – almost a meal in itself! It is best made with fresh ripe tomatoes, but in the winter months, when the tomatoes are pale and rather tasteless, make it with canned tomatoes instead, but always use fresh basil.

1½ lb (675 g) ripe tomatoes, peeled (see page 24), seeded and chopped

5 fl oz (150 ml) good quality olive oil

1 large onion, peeled and chopped

6 garlic cloves, peeled and crushed

¼ teaspoon crushed chillies

12 fresh basil leaves, chopped

1 lb (450 g) stale wholewheat bread

2½ pints (1½ litres) stock

Salt and freshly ground pepper

For serving:

Olive oil

Grated Parmesan

Heat the oil in a soup pan and cook the onion, garlic and crushed chillies for 2 to 3 minutes.

Add the tomatoes and chopped basil leaves, cover and cook gently for about 5 minutes.

Add the stale bread, torn into small pieces and the stock. Season to taste.

Bring to the boil, cover and reduce the heat. Simmer very gently, stirring occasionally, for about 45 minutes to 1 hour.

Serve with more olive oil and grated Parmesan.

BEEF IN BAROLO WINE
Brasato al Barolo

Preparation
10 minutes

Marinate
12 hours

3½ Cooking
3 hours 30 mins Serves 6

3 lb (about 1.5 kg) beef suitable for roasting, such as topside, brisket or chuck roast, rolled and tied

1 large onion, peeled and sliced

2 large carrots, sliced

1 sprig rosemary, crumbled

2 bay leaves, crumbled

1 sprig parsley

1 bottle of Barolo wine

4 tablespoons olive oil

1 pint (about 600 ml) meat stock

Salt and freshly ground black pepper

Put the meat in a bowl with the vegetables and herbs, pour over the wine, cover and place in the refrigerator for about 12 hours or overnight, turning the meat once.

To cook the meat, remove it from the marinade and pat it dry. Reserve the marinade. In a pot large enough to hold all the ingredients, heat the oil and brown the meat on all sides.

When the meat is brown, pour over the marinade and add the stock, and the salt and pepper. Cover and simmer gently for 2½ hours, turning the meat every now and then.

Remove the meat from the pot and keep warm. Pour all the liquid and vegetables from the pot into a blender and liquidise.

Return the meat to the pot, pour the sauce over the meat through a sieve, pressing the pulp through with a wooden spoon. The sauce should come to at least halfway up the meat. Adjust the seasoning, cover and simmer over a very low heat for a further 1 hour, turning the meat once or twice.

If during cooking the sauce gets too thick, thin it with some wine or stock. If, at the end of the cooking time, it is too thin, remove the meat, keep it warm and reduce the sauce by cooking vigorously until the right consistency is achieved.

Serve with more Barolo wine!

FISH SOUP GENOA STYLE
Burrida alla Genovese

Preparation	45 minutes
Cooking	40 minutes

Serves 4 to 6

Pancetta is an Italian bacon cured with salt and spices, but not smoked. It is found in Italian foodstores and some supermarkets, but can be replaced by streaky bacon.

2-2½ lb (1-1.5 kg) various fish (whole and filletted) and shellfish: monkfish, cod, hake, huss, red mullet, grey mullet, mussels, prawns, clams..

2-3 squid, cleaned (see page 26) and sliced

3 tablespoons olive oil

2 oz (50 g) pancetta or streaky bacon, chopped

1 small onion, peeled and chopped

1 carrot, peeled and chopped

1 celery stalk, chopped

½ bulb of fennel, chopped

1 large garlic clove, peeled

6 sprigs parsley, chopped

4 anchovy fillets, chopped

1 x 14 oz (400 g) can Italian plum tomatoes, drained

8-10 fresh basil leaves, chopped

Salt and freshly ground black pepper

8 fl oz (230 ml) dry white wine

1 pint (about 600 ml) water (approx.)

Clean and remove the heads of the whole fish and cut into pieces. Cut the fish fillets into chunks. Carefully wash and beard the mussels. Wash the prawns and the clams.

In a pan large enough to contain all the fish, heat the olive oil and gently fry the pancetta or bacon. Then add the onion and let it brown slightly. Add the carrot, celery, fennel, whole garlic clove, parsley and anchovy fillets. Cook together for about 5 minutes on a medium to low heat, stirring occasionally.

Then add the tomatoes, basil, salt and pepper to taste, wine, water and the squid, and leave to simmer gently for 10 to 15 minutes.

Add the pieces of fish, the mussels, prawns and clams. Stir and leave to simmer for another 10 to 15 minutes.

Meanwhile, toast or fry the slices of bread and arrange them in each soup plate. Set the fish and shellfish on top, ladle some of the cooking broth over each and serve immediately.

POLENTA WITH SAUSAGES
Polenta con salsicce

  Preparation 10 minutes

Cooking 45 minutes   Serves 6

For this dish, you need to make the polenta less solid by adding a little more water. It should have the consistency of mashed potatoes. Pork, beef or venison sausages are equally good to use.

8 oz (225 g) polenta (see page 25)	
2 fl oz (50 ml) olive oil	
12 Italian pork sausages	
2 pints (1.15 litres) rich tomato sauce (see page 26)	
2 oz (50 g) freshly grated Parmesan	

Prepare the polenta.

While the polenta is cooking, brown the sausages in the oil in a large frying pan, on a very low heat.

Make the tomato sauce.

When the polenta is ready, pile it up on a platter. Arrange the cooked sausages on top and pour over some of the tomato sauce. Sprinkle with Parmesan and serve.

Serve the rest of the tomato sauce separately.

POLENTA RING WITH CHICKEN LIVERS
Anello di polenta con fegatini di pollo

Preparation 20 minutes

Cooking 15 minutes   Serves 4 to 6

13 oz (375 g) polenta (see page 25)	
2 tablespoons olive oil	
4 oz (100 g) pancetta (see fish soup page 13) or bacon, diced	
4 oz (100 g) butter	
12 oz (350 g) mushrooms, finely sliced	
1 lb (450 g) chicken livers, cut into quarters	
½ teaspoon dry sage or 1 teaspoon chopped fresh sage	
1 level tablespoon plain flour	
8 fl oz (230 ml) dry white wine	
Salt and freshly ground black pepper	

Prepare the polenta. Butter a 9 to 10 inch (23 to 26 cm) ring mould and fill it with the polenta. Cover with foil and place the ring mould in a baking dish half filled with water. Place in a very low oven to keep warm while you cook the chicken liver sauce.

Heat the oil in a large pan and brown the diced pancetta or bacon. Add the butter and when it has melted, add the mushrooms and cook, stirring all the time, for about 2 minutes.

Then add the chicken livers and the sage. Sauté over a medium heat, until they are just brown. Sprinkle the flour over the livers, stir well to combine it with the juices, then add the wine. Stir and cook gently for about 3 to 4 minutes to make a rich sauce - do not overcook.

Remove the polenta from the oven and turn it out on to a warm platter. Pour the sauce of chicken livers into the centre and serve immediately.

LAMB AND BLACK OLIVE STEW
Agnello con olive nere

Preparation
20 minutes

Cooking
2 hours 30 mins **Serves 4**

2 lb (about 1 kg) boneless shoulder of lamb

4 tablespoons olive oil

2 large garlic cloves, peeled and crushed

2 sprigs fresh rosemary

8 fl oz (230 ml) dry white wine

1 lb (450 g) ripe tomatoes, peeled (see page 24), seeded and coarsely chopped

1 tablespoon grated lemon rind

Salt and freshly ground black pepper

6-7 oz (175-200 g) black olives, pitted and cut in half

Cut the lamb into 1 inch (2½ cm) cubes. Heat the oil in a large sauté pan and gently cook the garlic and the rosemary. When the garlic is golden, add the lamb cubes and brown them on all sides.

Add the wine and cook until it has almost evaporated. Then add the tomatoes, the grated lemon rind, salt and pepper to taste. Stir well, cover and cook on a low heat for 15 to 20 minutes.

Rinse and drain the olives and add them to the lamb. Cover and continue cooking very slowly for about 1½ to 2 hours, until the meat is tender. If the sauce begins to dry out during cooking, add some warm water.

Serve the meat and its sauce with boiled new potatoes, or slices of polenta (see page 25) fried in butter.

TAGLIATELLE WITH BOLOGNESE SAUCE
Tagliatelle alla Bolognese

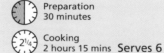 Preparation
30 minutes

Cooking
2 hours 15 mins **Serves 6**

Bolognese meat sauce, or Ragù, has travelled the world in one form or another. Even in Italy, each region has its own variation. You may use chicken liver; beef, pork or veal, or a combination of any of those, and the amount of tomato used depends on personal taste, but should never be overpowering. As ragù takes some time to cook, it can be prepared in advance, and stored in the refrigerator for a few days (or can be frozen) until needed.

1½ lb (675 g) Tagliatelle
2 tablespoons olive oil
2 tablespoons butter
3 oz (75 g) pancetta (see fish soup page 13) or bacon, finely chopped
2 medium-sized onions, peeled and finely chopped
2 celery stalks, finely chopped
2 medium-sized carrots, peeled and finely chopped
1½ lb (700 g) minced beef and veal, mixed
4 oz (100 g) chicken livers, finely chopped
8 fl oz (230 ml) dry white wine
5 tablespoons tomato purée
¾ pint (425 ml) warm meat stock
Salt and freshly ground black pepper
4 fl oz (120 ml) double cream
2 oz (50 g) grated Parmesan

In a large sauté pan, heat the oil and butter and brown the pancetta or bacon. Add the chopped onions, celery, carrots and sauté over a medium heat for 4 to 5 minutes.

Add the meat, breaking any lumps with a wooden spoon, and mix well with the vegetables. Cook until the meat is evenly browned. Then add the chicken livers, mix well and cook together for 3 to 4 minutes.

Add the wine and, when it has almost evaporated, stir in the tomato pureé mixed with 2 tablespoons of the stock. Add salt and pepper to taste and finally, add the rest of the stock. Bring to the boil, lower the heat, cover and simmer very gently for at least 2 hours, stirring occasionally.

If after 2 hours you find the sauce is too thin, simmer, uncovered, until it has reduced and thickened. Stir in the cream and continue to simmer until it is absorbed.

Finally cook your tagliatelle in boiling salted water with a little oil, until al dente. Serve with knobs of butter, the bolognese sauce on top and a sprinkling of grated Parmesan.

BOILED MEAT WITH GREEN SAUCE
Bollito misto con salsa verde

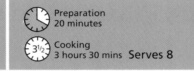

Preparation
20 minutes

Cooking
3 hours 30 mins **Serves 8**

Bollito is one of the great dishes of Northern Italy. Do not be put off by the term "boiled". Served with all the vegetables, the green sauce, various mustards or a spicy tomato sauce and, of course, some hearty red wine, it makes a great family or special occasion meal. The broth can be saved and served at another time.

2 lb (900 g) beef, brisket or silver side, rolled and tied with strings

1 x 1 lb (450 g) pig's trotter (optional)

1 lb (450 g) veal (optional)

1 small calf's tongue

4 onions, peeled and cut in half

2 carrots, peeled and cut in half

2 celery stalks, cut in half

4 sprigs of parsley

6 black peppercorns

Salt to taste

1 x 3 lb (1.4 kg) chicken

1 x 1-1½ lb (450-650 g) cotechino sausage, precooked

For the green sauce (salsa verde):

4 oz (100 g) fresh parsley

6 garlic cloves, peeled

4 oz (100 g) capers, drained

4 anchovy fillets (optional)

Juice of 1 lemon

4 fl oz (120 ml) virgin olive oil

Salt and freshly ground black pepper

Place the beef, (and any other meats, if using), and the tongue in a large saucepan with all the vegetables and parsley, cover with water, add the salt and the peppercorns. Cover, bring to the boil, then turn the heat down and simmer gently.

After about 2½ hours, add the chicken and continue to simmer the meats gently for a further 1 hour, or until the meats and chicken are cooked.

Heat the cotechino sausage in a separate saucepan in simmering water for about 20 to 30 minutes.

Meanwhile, prepare the green sauce (salsa verde). Place the parsley, garlic, capers and anchovies, if used, in the food processor bowl and chop finely. Empty into a bowl, add the lemon juice and the oil, season and stir well. The sauce should be quite thick.

Just before serving, remove the tongue and take off its skin and any bits of gristle. Return it to the pan to warm through again.

To serve, slice the meats and the cotechino sausage and place on a large platter with the chicken. Serve with the green sauce and the cooking stock.

RISOTTO WITH SAFFRON AND PARMESAN CHEESE
Risotto alla Milanese

Preparation 10 minutes

Cooking 25 minutes

Serves 4

Italy is the biggest producer of rice in Europe and the Po valley boasts no less than 4 different varieties. The best rice for a risotto is the Arborio, a short round grain. The bone marrow is not essential for this dish, but it does add richness to it.

2½ pints (1½ litres) meat stock

4 oz (100 g) butter

1 small onion, finely chopped

2 oz (50 g) pancetta (see page 13) or bone marrow, finely chopped

½ lb (225 g) risotto rice

¼ pint (150 ml) dry white wine

1 generous pinch of saffron powder (or saffron threads)

Salt and freshly ground black pepper

2 oz (50 g) freshly grated Parmesan

Bring the stock to a simmer and keep it simmering slowly. Put the saffron powder or threads to soak in 2 tablespoons of the hot stock.

Heat half the butter in a heavy pan, add the onion and pancetta, or bone marrow, and cook until the onion is soft and transparent.

Add the rice, stir well to coat the rice with the butter. Pour in the wine and a ladle of the simmering stock. Stirring frequently, cook over a moderate heat, uncovered, adding some hot stock when the liquid has been absorbed.

Add the saffron after about 15 minutes and mix well. Continue cooking and adding stock until the rice is cooked (about 20 minutes). The risotto should be creamy and the grains tender but firm to the bite.

Remove from the heat, season to taste and mix in the Parmesan and remaining butter. Stir well and serve.

VENETIAN RICE AND PEAS
Risi e Bisi

Preparation 40 minutes

Cooking 30 minutes

Serves 6 to 8

Risi e Bisi is a classic dish that dates back to the days of the Doges of Venice. It would be served at the banquets to celebrate the Feast of St Mark. Although it is sometimes classed as a soup, it is always served thick enough to eat with a fork.

1 lb (450 g) Italian risotto rice

2 oz (50 g) butter

1 tablespoon olive oil

3 tablespoons finely chopped fresh parsley

1 small onion, peeled and finely chopped

5 oz (150 g) cooked ham, diced

1 lb (450 g) fresh shelled peas

4 pints (2.3 litres) meat stock

Salt and freshly ground black pepper

2 oz (50 g) butter

2 oz (50 g) grated Parmesan

Bring the stock to a simmer and keep it simmering gently.

In a large heavy pan with a lid, gently heat the butter and oil, add the rice and parsley, and mix well to coat the grains with the oil and butter.

Add the onion and the ham and cook for a few minutes, until the onion is soft and transparent. Add the peas and about 2 pints of the hot stock. Mix well, cover

and cook on a low heat for 20 to 30 minutes, stirring occasionally, adding some of the remaining hot stock when the liquid has been absorbed.

When cooked, the rice should be creamy and the grains tender but still firm to the bite. Add salt and pepper to taste. Dot with knobs of butter and sprinkle with grated Parmesan.